© Aladdin Books Ltd 2001

Designed and produced by
Aladdin Books Ltd
28 Percy Street
London W1P 0LD

First published in
Great Britain in 2001 by
Franklin Watts
96 Leonard Street
London EC2A 4XD

ISBN 0 7496 4165 7

Printed in Belgium

Editor
Bibby Whittaker

Literacy Consultant
Jackie Holderness
Westminster Institute of Education,
Oxford Brookes University

Design
Flick, Book Design and Graphics

Picture Research
Brian Hunter Smart

Illustration
Mary Lonsdale for SGA

Picture Credits
Abbreviations: t – top, m – middle,
b – bottom, r – right, l – left, c – centre.
All photographs supplied by Select
Pictures except for Cover, 2tl, 5, 11 –
Digital Stock. 4tl, 6tl, 6-7, 12tl, 14tl,
15, 19tr, 23tr, 23mr, 23br – Stockbyte.
9, 20tl – Corbis. 13, 23ml – Corbis
Royalty Free. 16 – Rowland Dowling
/CORBIS. 18-19 – John Foxx Images.

READING ABOUT

Colours

By Jim Pipe

Aladdin/Watts
London • Sydney

Blue

Jo gets up and sees the snow.

She wants to go out and play.

So she puts on her clothes.

What colour is Jo's vest?
It is blue like a peacock.

It is blue like the sea and
the sky on a sunny day.

Red

What colour are Jo's socks?

Jo wants red socks today.

Red like a tomato.

Very hot things turn red.

This volcano is red hot!

 # Yellow

Did you see Jo's yellow socks?

They are yellow like a banana.

Jo likes yellow.

It feels warm like the sun.

So Jo puts on a yellow shirt.

Orange

What colour are Jo's jeans?

Jo's jeans are orange.

Orange like a pumpkin.

Armbands are also orange.

Orange is easy to see.

Purple

What colour
is Jo's jumper?

Jo's jumper
is purple.

Purple like
a grape.

Jo's grandma loves purple. She has purple flowers in her garden.

Green

What colour are Jo's boots and hat?

They are all green.

Jo's boots are dark green.

Her hat is light green, like a pea.

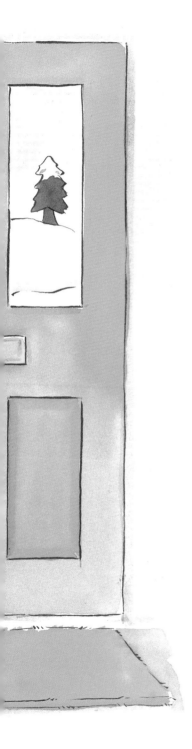

This green frog is
sitting on a green leaf.

Which is light green
and which is dark?

Brown

What colour is Jo's coat?

Jo's coat is brown like a nut.

It is brown like a tree trunk.

This moth is brown, too.
When it sits on a tree,
it is hard to see.

Black and white

What colour is Jo's scarf?

It is black and white.

It has stripes like a zebra.

Jo's dog is black and white, too.

But it has spots!

Grey

What colour are Jo's gloves?

Jo's gloves are grey.
Grey like an
elephant.

Grey is a mix of
black and white.

Black and white
clouds make
the sky grey.

19

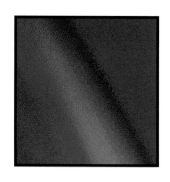

Lots of colours

Jo is wearing lots of colours.

Bright colours like a rainbow.

Jo's friends like bright
colours, too.

How many colours can
you name?

Here are the colours in this book.

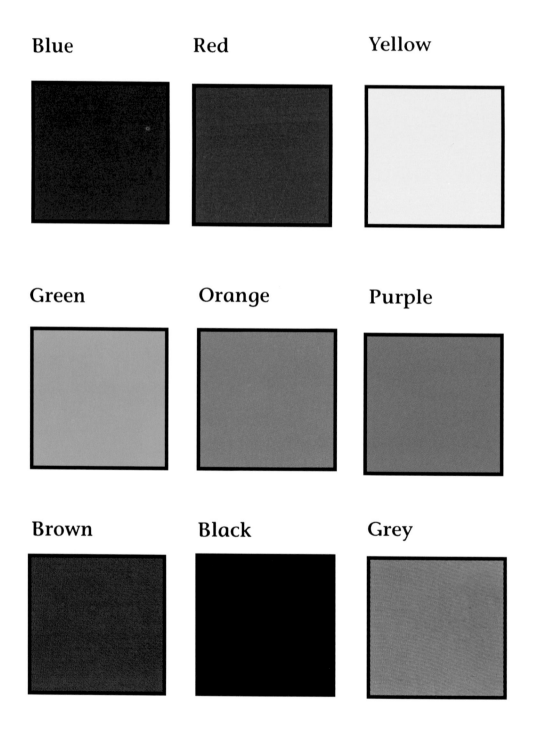

Blue

Red

Yellow

Green

Orange

Purple

Brown

Black

Grey

What colours are these things?

Sea

Scarf

Sock

Frog

Sun

Nuts

Can you make
a story with
these words?

Do you know?

You can mix paint colours.

Red + Blue = Purple

Yellow + Blue = Green

Red + Yellow = Orange

Colours can be light or dark.

Light Blue   **Dark Blue**